get started in

PAINT
POURING

Easy Techniques, Awesome Ideas, & Inspiration for Absolute Beginners

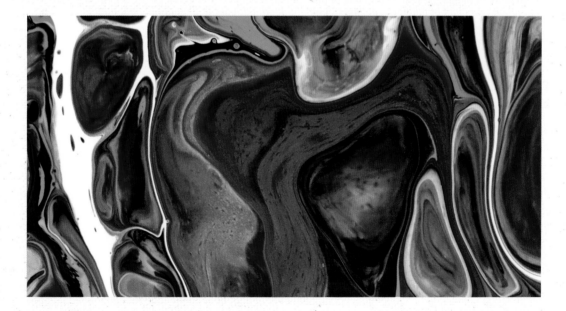

LEISURE ARTS, INC. • Maumelle, Arkansas

table of CONTENTS

PAINT POURING

Welcome to Paint Pouring

In this book, we will teach you how to start creating your own mesmerizing fluid art by using techniques tailored for artists of any level. We will share our secrets to the Perfect Pour so that you, too, can enjoy the addictive, meditative and relaxing art of Paint Pouring.

MATERIALS

Basic Supplies

- ☐ Acrylic Paint
- ☐ Pouring Medium for Thinning the Paints for Pouring
- ☐ Cups for Mixing and Pouring
- ☐ Craft Sticks for Stirring
- ☐ Freezer Paper or Plastic Sheeting for Protecting Your Surfaces
- ☐ Canvas or Other Appropriate Item to Pour On
- ☐ Paper Towels

Optional Supplies

- ☐ Additives like 100% Silicone Oil, Dimethicone, or Isopropyl Alcohol
- ☐ Pipettes
- ☐ Gloves
- ☐ Apron
- ☐ Push pins
- ☐ Painter's Tape

FAQS

What kind of paint should I use? Acrylic. You can use acrylic paints of any grade and viscosity with varying effects. Soft body acrylics, fluid acrylics and craft paints will be the easiest to work with, while heavy body paints will need extra care to thin.

What's a pouring medium? A medium is something that is mixed with the paint in order to change a paint's consistency without altering the color or the ability to bind. Most mediums are white, but dry clear. In paint pouring, we use a pouring medium that will allow us to thin the paints for pouring. There are brand name, commercially made pouring medium products, as well as many DIY recipes available online that include products like glue and paint conditioners.

What's an additive? Do I need to use one? We use additives to help create cells and other effects. Cells, or the "bubbly effect," happen when colors peek through other layers of color. Using an additive is optional. Additives used in Paint Pouring include silicone oils, dimethicone and isopropyl alcohol. They are added to the paint separately from the pouring medium.

How long does it take to dry? In most cases your painting will be dry to the touch within 24 hours, but it can sometimes take longer. Temperature, humidity and how thick your paint is left on the canvas can affect drying time.

What can I pour on? Stretched canvas and cradled wood panels are the most popular, but you can pour paint on lots of other things. Ceramic tiles, synthetic papers, paper maché, mixed media papers, vinyl records, cds, rocks and furniture. There are many more possibilities!

What's a dirty cup, and why are we flipping it? A dirty cup is just a cup with multiple colors of paint poured or layered into it. When you "flip" the cup upside down onto your substrate, it is called a "flip cup." This is just one of many pouring techniques that artists use to create fluid art.

What's "Flooding the Canvas" mean? Flooding the canvas is when a solid base color, oftentimes white, is poured over the entire canvas. This base coating of wet paint helps to improve flow of the paint colors that are flipped or poured over the top of it. It can also create interesting effects and areas of negative space, depending on the technique used.

What do I do with all the paint that is tilted off the canvas or drips off the sides? Any paint that drips off onto the freezer paper when dry can be peeled off as a "skin" and saved to use in other projects like jewelry and collages. Also, mini canvases, wood circle cutouts and ceramic tiles can be dipped into the overflow paint for quick smaller works of art.

HELPFUL HINTS

- Painting surfaces should be level, so that the paint settles and dries evenly. There are many smart phone apps that can assist you with leveling if you don't have a real level on hand.
- Start with the white paint when layering paint colors in the cups. White is one of the heaviest paints. When the cup is flipped the white paint will end up on top and will then drop down through the other colors helping to create different tints of colors.
- A box can be used to cover the finished, still wet canvas while drying to keep dust, dander and curious fingers from settling in the paint before it's completely dry.
- Painter's tape can be used to cover the back of the canvas frame to keep it clean of paint.

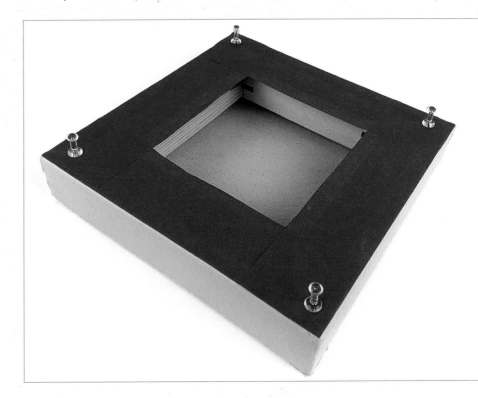

- Push-pins inserted on the backside of each corner of the canvas frame will help elevate the canvas and keep it up and out of the tilted off paint.
- It's important to keep your canvas elevated and not left to sit in wet paint while drying. If not using push-pins, an upturned cup under each corner will work just as well to lift the canvas, so that air can circulate around it while drying.

how to prepare
PAINTS FOR POURING

SHOPPING LIST

- ☐ Acrylic Paint - 1 fluid ounce
- ☐ Pouring Medium - 4 fluid ounces
- ☐ Water
- ☐ Plastic Pipette
- ☐ Craft Sticks for Stirring
- ☐ Cups for Mixing
- ☐ 100% Silicone Oil (optional)

INSTRUCTIONS

1 • Add 4 parts pouring medium to 1 part acrylic paint.

2 • Mix paint and pouring medium together slowly and thoroughly to reduce bubbles and ensure consistency.

3 • Paint when mixed should be the consistency of warm honey. It should fall from the stir stick in a single stream without breaking.

4 • There should be a small build-up on the surface as the paint falls and then the paint should quickly smooth out.

5 • Should the mixture be too thick and not the consistency of warm honey when well mixed, water can be added a few drops at a time until it is. If your mixture is too thin add some additional paint.

6 • The optional last step is to add an additive like 100% silicone oil. Add 2 drops per 5 fluid ounces of paint. Mix well.

Keep in mind that the ratio of paint to pouring medium may have to be modified depending on the particular acrylic paint and pouring medium being used. Paint density varies across brand, type and the individual color being used. Even the weather can affect the thickness of the paints. For example, white is very heavy and requires extra attention when mixing. Use our 1 part paint to 4 parts pouring medium as a starting point, but don't be afraid to play with the amounts to get the right consistency that works for you and the products you choose to pour with. Part of the excitement of paint pouring is experimenting!

Canvas Size	Prepared Paint Amount Per Canvas Size	Canvas Size	Prepared Paint Amount Per Canvas Size
4" x 4"	5 fl. oz.	16" x 20"	25 fl. oz.
5" x 5"	6 fl. oz.	18" x 24"	33 fl. oz.
6" x 6"	7 fl. oz.	20" x 20"	32 fl. oz.
8" x 8"	8 fl. oz.	20" x 24"	38 fl. oz.
8" x 10"	9 fl. oz.	22" x 28"	47 fl. oz.
9" x 12"	10 fl. oz.	24" x 24"	45 fl. oz.
10" x 10"	9 fl. oz.	24" x 30"	55 fl. oz.
10" x 12"	10 fl. oz.	24" x 36"	65 fl. oz.
11" x 14"	12 fl. oz.	30" x 40"	89 fl. oz.
12" x 12"	12 fl. oz.	36" x 36"	95 fl. oz.
12" x 16"	16 fl. oz.	36" x 48"	126 fl. oz.
12" x 36"	33 fl. oz.	48" x 48"	168 fl. oz.
14" x 18"	22 fl. oz.	48" x 60"	210 fl. oz.
15" x 30"	35 fl. oz.		*Amounts are approximate.*

DIRTY POUR
technique

SHOPPING LIST

- ☐ (1) - 8" x 8" Canvas
- ☐ (4) - 3 fl. oz. Cups
- ☐ (1) - 8 fl. oz. Cup
- ☐ (4) - Acrylic Paints Prepared For Pouring (see page 8)
  - • 2 fl. oz. Aqua Green
  - • 2 fl. oz. Cobalt Blue
  - • 2 fl. oz. Magenta
  - • 2 fl. oz. White
- ☐ 100% Silicone Oil - 1 Drop Per Color

INSTRUCTIONS

1 • Add prepared paints in the cup starting with white. Alternate paint colors in differing amounts. Colors added to the cup do not have to be in any particular order.

2 • After adding all the paint, insert a stir stick into the paint and sweep it from one side of the cup to the other, once in each direction, +. This will help to mix the paints slightly.

3 • Remove stir stick and set aside.

DIRTY POUR *technique*

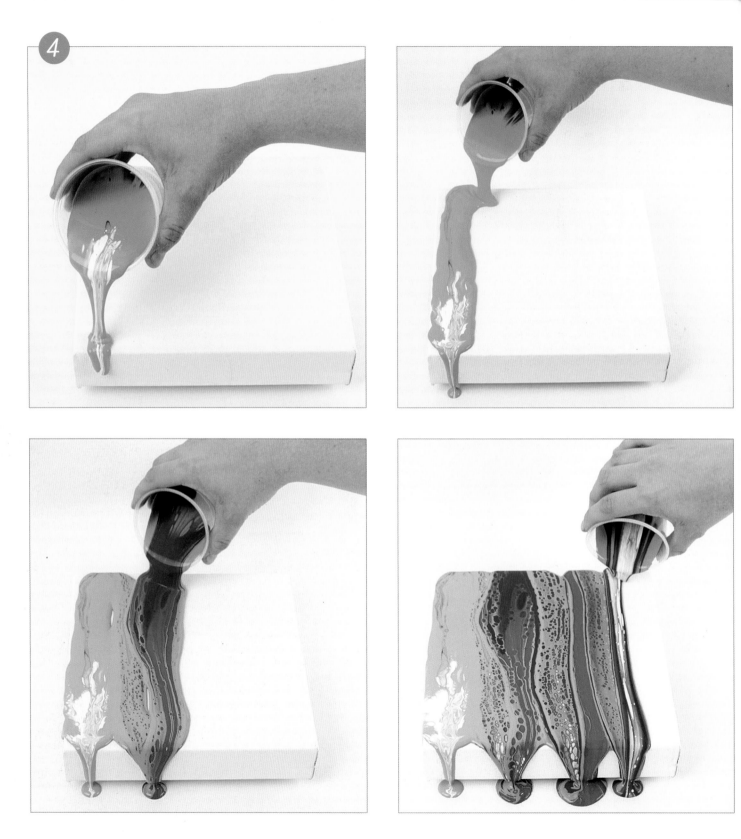

4 • Starting at one corner, slowly pour paint from one end to the other, until the canvas is covered.

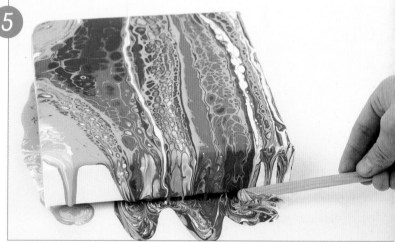

5 • A stir stick can be used to pick up paint drippings and cover the sides of the canvas where the paint didn't cover.

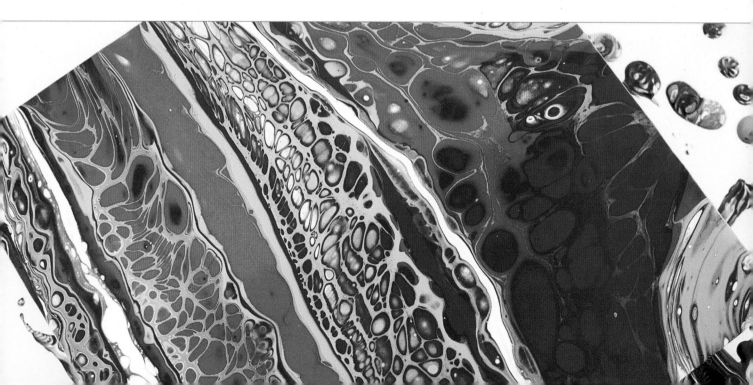

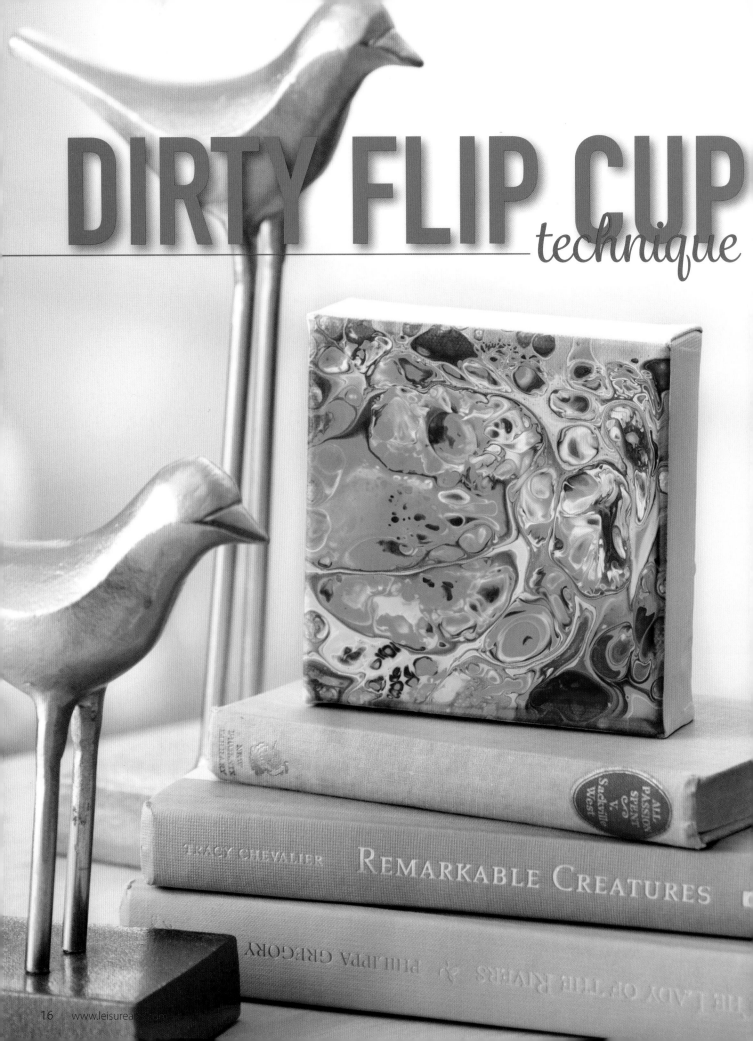

DIRTY FLIP CUP *technique*

SHOPPING LIST

- ☐ (1) - 5" x 5" Canvas
- ☐ (4) - 3 fl. oz. Cups
- ☐ (1) - 5 fl. oz. Cup
- ☐ (4) - Acrylic Paints Prepared For Pouring (see page 8)
  - • 2 fl. oz. Aqua Green
  - • 2 fl. oz. Magenta
  - • 2 fl. oz. White
  - • 2 fl. oz. Yellow
- ☐ 100% Silicone Oil - 1 Drop Per Color

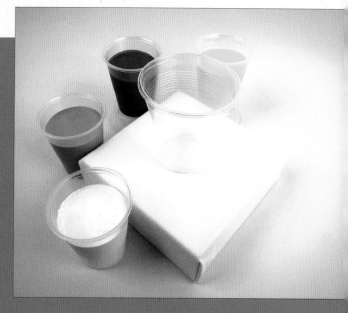

INSTRUCTIONS

1 • Add prepared paints in the cup starting with white.

2 • Alternate paint colors in differing amounts.

3 • Colors added to the cup do not have to be in any particular order.

Flipping The Cup Onto The Canvas

4 • Place canvas on top of cup.

DIRTY FLIP CUP *technique*

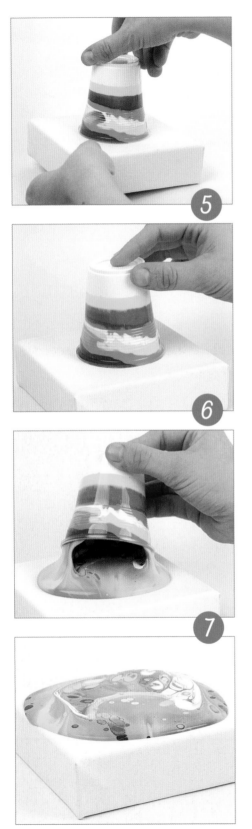

5 • Holding canvas and cup together, flip both over, so that the cup is now upside down on top of canvas.

6 • Allow the cup of paint to settle for a few moments.

7 • Lift the cup and set empty cup aside.

8 • Tilt canvas until the paint covers the canvas.

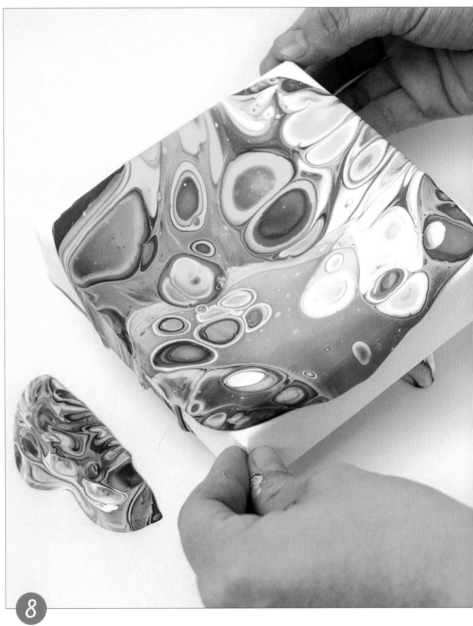

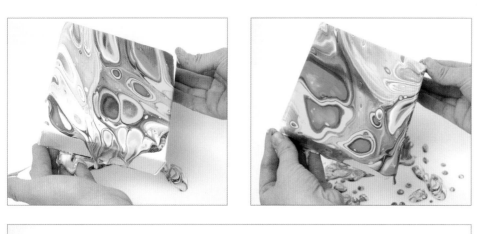

Look at the beautiful cells created in the paint!

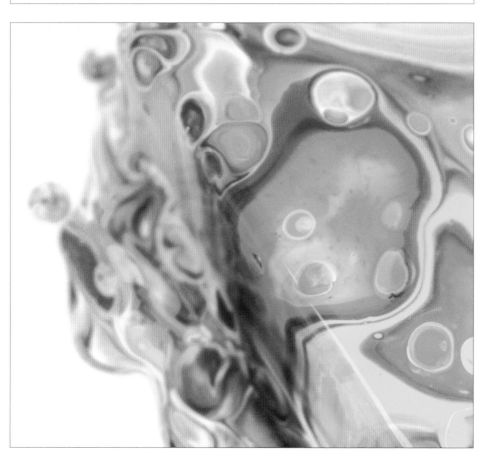

PUDDLE POUR
technique

SHOPPING LIST

- ☐ (1) - 8" x 8" Canvas
- ☐ (4) - 3 fl.oz. Cups
- ☐ (4) - Acrylic Paints Prepared For Pouring (see page 8)
  - 2 fl.oz. Magenta
  - 2 fl.oz. Light Blue
  - 2 fl.oz. Purple
  - 2 fl.oz. White

INSTRUCTIONS

1 • A puddle pour involves pouring paint colors one on top of the other. Alternate the colors one at a time allowing the colors to spread out across the surface.

PUDDLE POUR *technique*

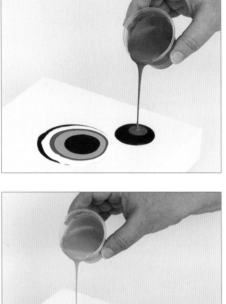

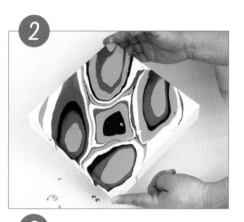

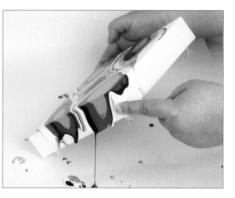

2 • Tilt canvas until a desirable composition is achieved.

3 • Use a stir stick and leftover paint to cover any bare canvas.

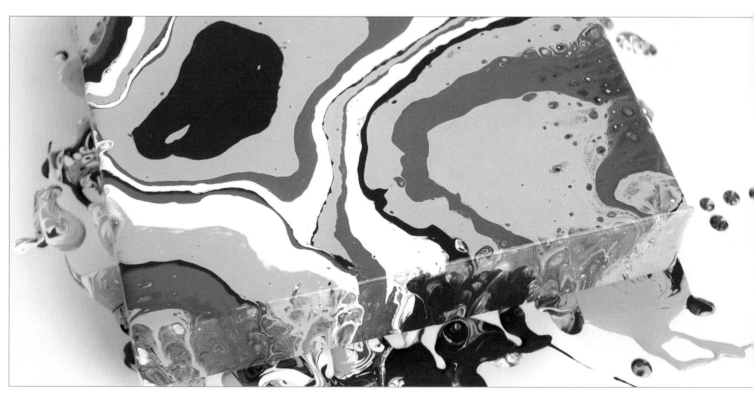

SWIPE

technique

SHOPPING LIST

- ☐ (1) - 8" x 8" Canvas
- ☐ (7) - 3 fl. oz. Cups
- ☐ (7) - Acrylic Paints Prepared For Pouring (see page 8)
  - • 2 fl. oz. Red
  - • 2 fl. oz. Orange
  - • 2 fl. oz. Yellow
  - • 2 fl. oz. Green
  - • 2 fl. oz. Blue
  - • 2 fl. oz. Purple
  - • 2 fl. oz. White
- ☐ 100% Silicone Oil - 1 Drop Per Color
- ☐ Paper Towels

INSTRUCTIONS

In this demonstration we use a wet paper towel to swipe with, but there are many other items that can be used as well. Some of the popular tools used for swiping are transparency film sheets, crafts sticks, offset spatulas, fondant smoother, old credit cards, rulers, pieces of cardboard from mailers and packaging.

1 • Pour each cup of prepared paint across the canvas in a "rainbow" color order.

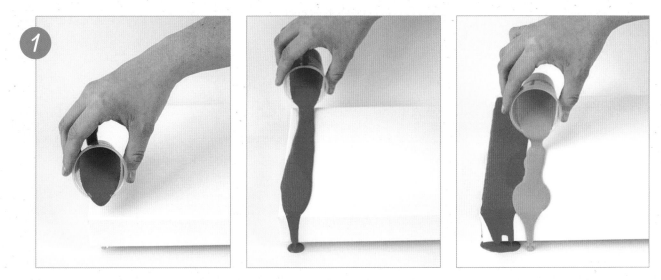

SWIPE *technique*

  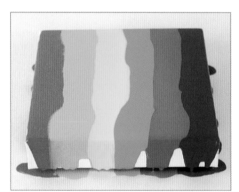

2 • Pour white paint 1" from the edge, horizontally across the top of the canvas.

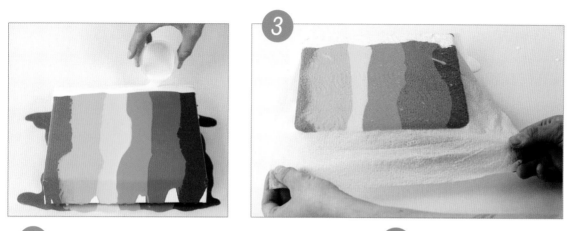

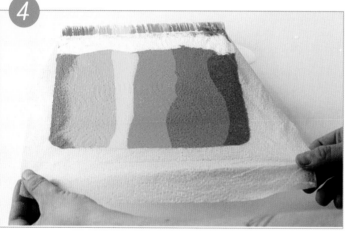

3 • Place a wet paper towel over the top of the canvas

4 • Slowly pull the wet paper towel across the canvas, while dragging the white paint over the other colors. Keep the end of the paper towel being held slightly elevated.

5 • Continue pulling the paper towel until the white paint reaches the edge and proceeds to drip down the side. Set aside the paper towel.

6 • If desired, the canvas can now be tilted until the paint covers the edges. If needed, use a craft stick to pick up excess paint to cover the sides.

27

SWIRL POUR
technique
(TREE RING)

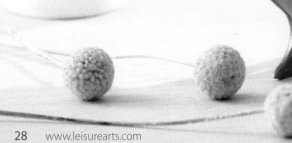

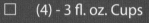

- ☐ (1) - 8" x 8" Canvas
- ☐ (4) - 3 fl. oz. Cups
- ☐ (1) - 8 fl. oz. Cup
- ☐ (4) - Acrylic Paints Prepared For Pouring
  (see page 8)
  - 2 fl. oz. Blue Green
  - 2 fl. oz. Blue
  - 2 fl. oz. Yellow Green
  - 6 fl. oz. White

INSTRUCTIONS

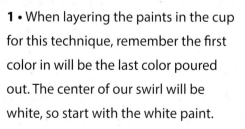

1 • When layering the paints in the cup for this technique, remember the first color in will be the last color poured out. The center of our swirl will be white, so start with the white paint.

2 • Pour the prepared paints in the cup in random order. Pour the paints from near the top of the cup. This will encourage less mixing of the colors. If the paint is poured from high above the cup, the paint colors will mix together more.

SWIRL POUR (TREE RING) *technique*

3 • End your pouring with blue so the outer swirl will be blue.

Flooding The Canvas

4 • Pour white paint in the center of the canvas. Tilt the canvas until white paint covers the surface.

5 • Start pouring the layered dirty cup onto the center of the wet paint-covered canvas.

6 • As the paint falls from the cup, slightly swirl the cup. This swirling motion will help to create rings in the paint as it moves out and covers the canvas.

7 • Tilt the canvas until you are happy with the placement.

FLIP & DRAG
technique

SHOPPING LIST

- ☐ (1) - 8" x 8" Canvas
- ☐ (4) - 3 fl. oz. Cups
- ☐ (1) - 5 fl. oz. Cup
- ☐ (4) - Acrylic Paints Prepared For Pouring (see page 8)
  - 2 fl. oz. Blue
  - 2 fl. oz. Purple
  - 2 fl. oz. Yellow Green
  - 5 fl. oz. White
- ☐ 100% Silicone Oil - 1 Drop Per Color, Except White

INSTRUCTIONS

1 • Add prepared paints in the cup starting with white. Alternate the paint colors in differing amounts.

FLIP & DRAG *technique*

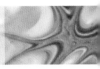

2 • Pour white paint in the center of the canvas. Use a stir stick to spread the paint over the canvas.

Flipping The Cup Onto The Canvas

3 • Place a scrap piece of cardboard on top of cup.

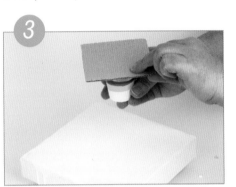
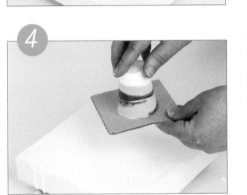

4 • Flip cup and cardboard over.

5 • Slide cup off of cardboard onto the canvas.

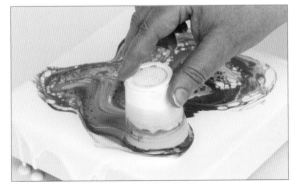

7 • With a light touch slide the cup around the canvas.

6 • Using a push-pin, poke a hole in the bottom of the cup. This releases the pressure and enables the cup to be moved around the surface easier.

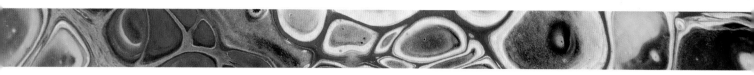

8 • Tilt the canvas to help move the paint across the surface.

9 • Lift the cup and set empty cup aside.

GALLERY

Like most people, I've been inspired by a number of Artists, many of which can be found sharing their work on social media sites. The paint pouring community online is large, active and very welcoming!

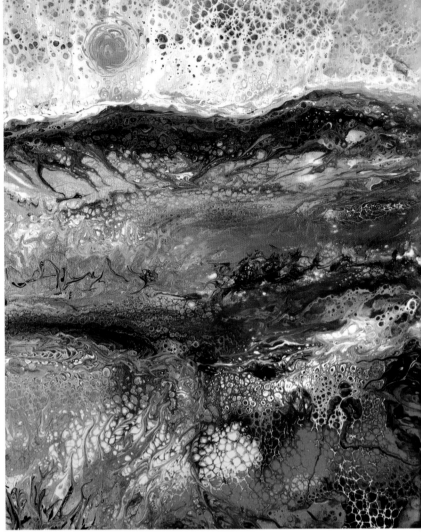

Caren Goodrich

Caren Goodrich is a lifelong artist, currently focusing on acrylic pouring and resin pours. Her extensive art background has enabled her to combine knowledge from other art mediums into the exciting world of paint pouring. You can find her video tutorials about paint pouring at http://www.youtube.com/carengoodrich.

You Tube Caren Goodrich
f Caren Goodrich Art
○ carengoodrich

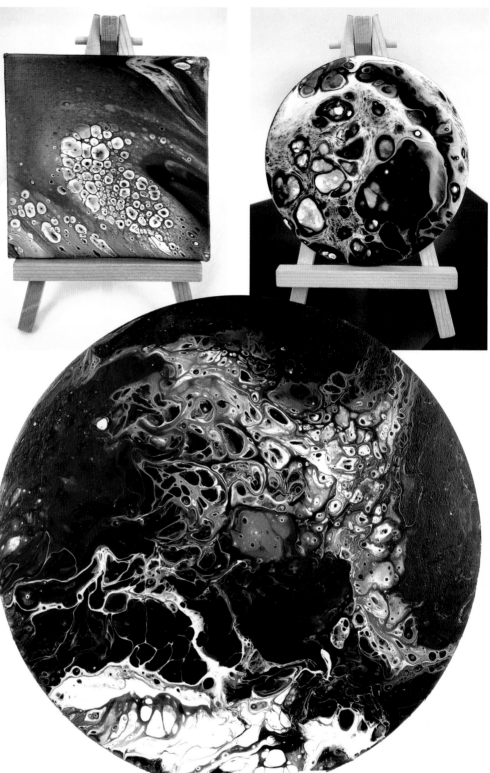

Lauren LaRee Burch

Lauren LaRee Burch is a California born, Texas-raised artist who specializes in surrealism and fluid abstract art. She draws her inspiration from her dual Japanese and European heritages, nature, and her lifelong exposure to various art forms through her mother, Nicky James Burch.

Lauren launched LaRee Studio in 2011, painting surreal portraits in watercolor. She has since evolved and works in mixed media, including inks, acrylics, and graphite. She is studying Studio Arts at the University of North Texas and displays and sells her art both locally and nationally. She currently shares her work on the internet through Instagram and Facebook.

Lauren joined Fluid Art Studios in late 2017, and plays an active part in developing new techniques, reviewing products, and teaching others the magic of paint pouring.

When Lauren LaRee isn't painting, she is honing her craft as a Coffee Master, and spreading the joy of creativity with her two children, Kayla and Seamus.

You Tube LaRee Studio

f Laree Studio

lareestudio

37

Melissa Dion Murphy (MelyD)

Melissa Dion Murphy a.k.a. MelyD. artist, is an abstract and conceptual fluid painter presently located in Montréal, Québec. Using acrylic paint and artist products, she works towards controlled results and does nothing but impress. Her ability to create new ways of pouring and moving around the paint is truly inspiring. Her amazing color palettes can be seen throughout social media. She is known to shine with her down to earth personality and by showing her experiments on her YouTube Channel. She has helped thousands learn about fluid painting through her journey. You can purchase her work through her website at melydartist.com

You Tube MelyD.artist

f MelyD.artist

o melyd.artist

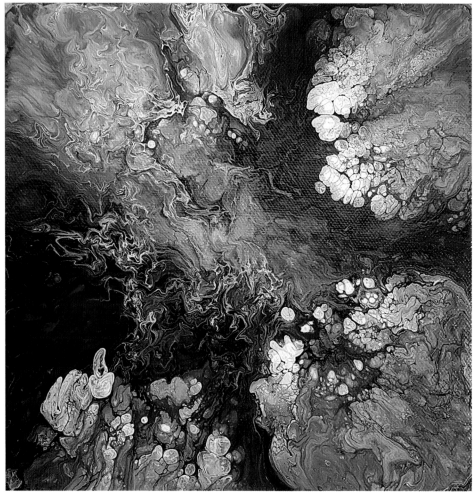

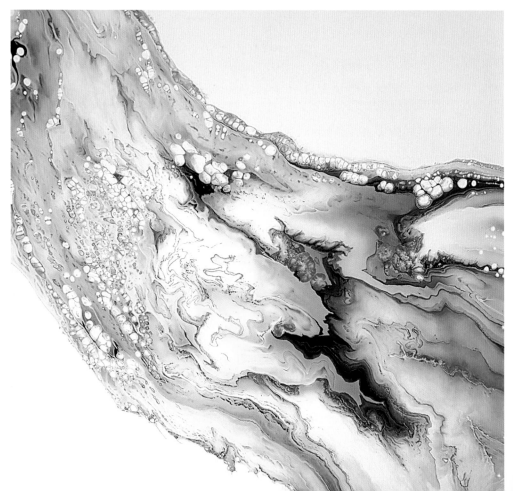

Rick Cheadle

Rick Cheadle is a self taught mixed-media artist specializing in acrylic paint pouring. Inspired by his long-standing fascination with Mid Century art and design compositions that he grew up with, Cheadle's expansive portfolio explores multiple mediums and styles including Abstract Expressionism, Color Field, Pop Art, and Mixed Media Sculptures.

Rick has been in the Creative Arts Industry since 1996. He is a passionate teacher with thousands of students all over the world. Teaching art to aspiring artists is his passion and lifelong dream. His work is collected world-wide and includes large-scale wall art pieces, commission works for The Johnny Cash Museum in Nashville, Tennessee, wall sculptures, found objects, as well as a plethora of mixed media works.

Multi-layered and full of vibrant colors, Rick Cheadle's artwork weaves tales of a beloved era in design and a unique blend of modern techniques to reignite our senses and fill our lives with beautiful dreamlike colorscapes.

You Tube Rick Cheadle
Cheadle Designs
rickcheadle

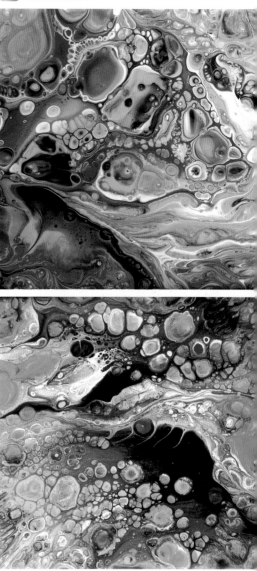

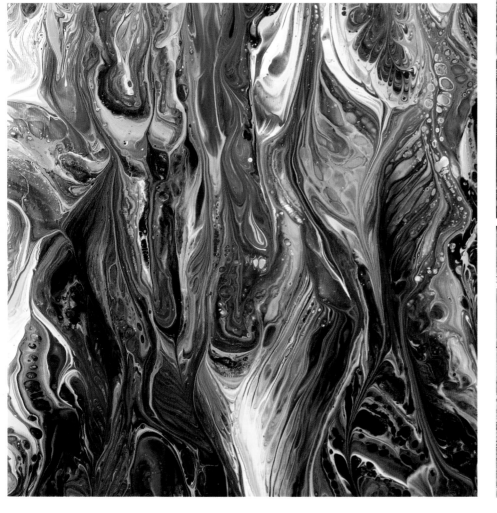

Rio & Saress

Rio (of the mother and son duo Rio and Saress) has been on a quest for color ever since she was given her first box of crayons. For the last 32 years, color is what has driven her to the many different subjects that she has painted. Everything is beautiful in its own way, and everything has a story that needs to be told, and for Rio the pen that tells that story is color.

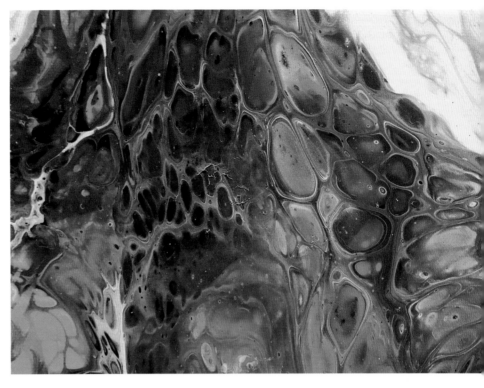

Rio has had the privilege of training with one of the Top Contemporary Masters in the modern art world specifically on color. For the last 5 years, Kay Griffith has continued to help Rio expand her knowledge base of what color is and what and how to manipulate it to flow the way the canvas needs it to flow. As a result of this training, paint pouring has become a natural extension of what she has learned. It has offered a unique way to stretch the boundaries of color and really submerge the senses into the canvas. For Rio, paint pouring is a relaxing way to experiment with the pigment. It has become yet another facet of her desire to master every hue.

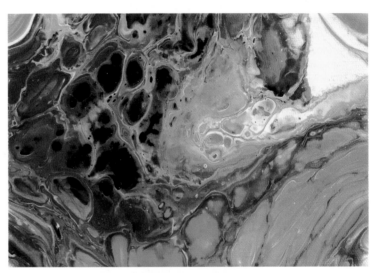

riosaressgallery@gmail.com

www.riosaressgallery.com

You Tube Rio Saress

Rio Saress

rioandsace

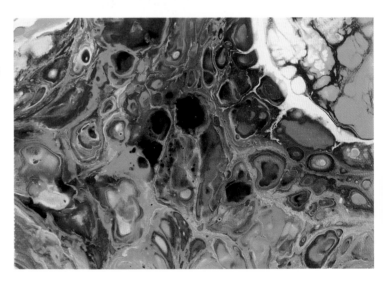

Ann Osborne

Ann Osborne is an abstract artist who loves to share her excitement about painting and creating art in general. She has a successful YouTube channel (Ann Osborne) which has added a fun, new direction in her art. With a background in mixed media and mosaic art, she has found her niche in fluid painting. The balance between controlling the paint while letting the paint flow on its own appeals to the sense of freedom she desires in her art. The technique she utilizes the most is one which she has coined the "flip and drag". Negative white space is a constant theme in her art, and the other colors she uses depend on which ones call out to her the most that day. Along with painting, she is an educator of teenagers with special needs, and is a wife and mother of two.

You**Tube** Ann Osborne ⬛ annosborne76
f Ann Osborne Art

Bianca Gaspard

Bianca Gaspard is an artist, wife and mother. She has been doing some type of crafting off and on her entire life. She is a self taught artist who loves making things with her hands, the messier the better. Bianca taught paper crafting classes for three years at a scrapbook store in Tucson, AZ and is always up to trying something new.

You**Tube** Bianca Gaspard
f Rambling Crafter
⬛ ramblingcrafter

CALYPSO
coasters

SHOPPING LIST

- ☐ (4) - 4" x 4" Bisque Plain Ceramic Coasters
- ☐ (4) - 3 fl.oz. Cups
- ☐ (1) - 5 fl.oz. Cup
- ☐ (4) - Acrylic Paints Prepared For Pouring (see page 8)
  - 2 fl.oz. Turquoise
  - 2 fl.oz. Blue Green
  - 2 fl.oz. Iridescent Gold
  - 5 fl.oz. White
- ☐ Drinking Straw
- ☐ 100% Silicone Oil - 1 Drop Per Color, Except White
- ☐ Optional: Cork and adhesive.

INSTRUCTIONS

1 • Layer the prepared paints. Paints can be added in a random order with differing amounts of paint.

CALYPSO *coasters*

2 • Place the coasters side by side. Cover the surface with white paint.

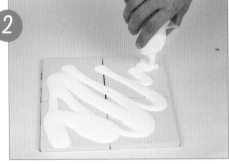

3 • Slowly pour layered paint across the coasters. Using a straw, blow paint out and over the white paint.

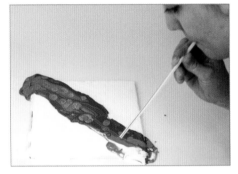

4 • Tilt the canvas to help move the paint across the surface.

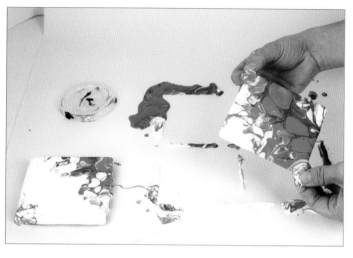

5 • Elevate each coaster on a upturned cup and leave to dry for 24-48 hours.

6 • Cut cork to size of each coaster and glue to backs.

FOCAL POINT *frames*

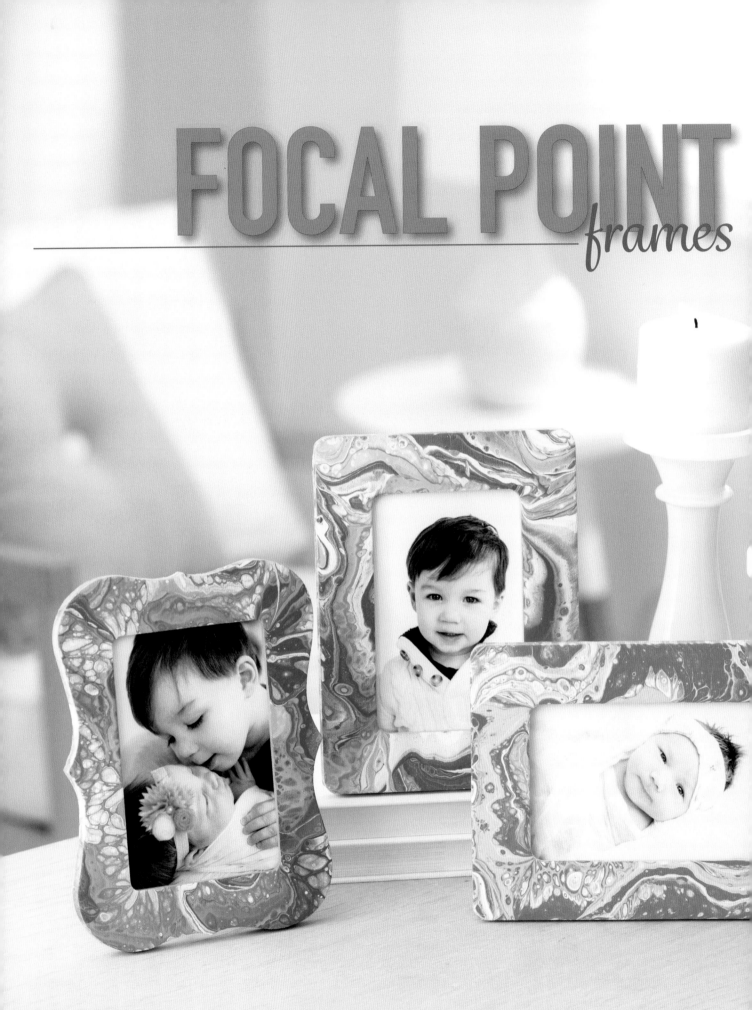

SHOPPING LIST

- ☐ (1) - Wooden frame for a 4" x 6" photo
- ☐ (3) - 3 fl. oz. Cups
- ☐ (1) - 5 fl. oz. Cup
- ☐ (4) - Acrylic Paints Prepared For Pouring (see page 8)
  - • 2 fl. oz. Magenta
  - • 2 fl. oz. Light Pink
  - • 2 fl. oz. White
- ☐ 100% Silicone Oil - 1 Drop Per Color
- ☐ Painter Tape and 1 oz. Condiment Cups

INSTRUCTIONS

1 • Tape off the back of the frame to keep it clean while pouring.

2 • Elevate each corner of the frame on an upside down condiment cup to keep the frame lifted out of the paint overflow.

Preparing the Dirty Cup of Paint for Pouring

3 • Add prepared paints to cup starting with white to prepare a dirty cup of paint.

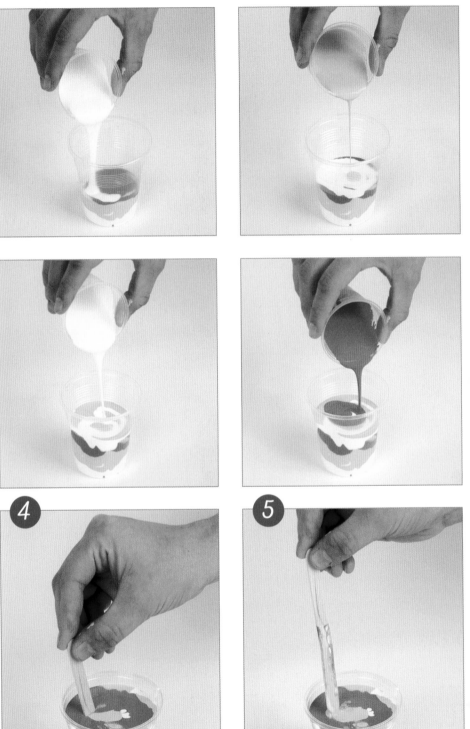

4 • Insert a stir stick into the paint cup and sweep it from one side of the cup to the other, once in each direction, +. This will slightly mingle the paints.

5 • Remove stir stick and set aside.

6 • Slowly pour the paint across the frame.

7 • Using a stir stick, cover any bare areas with the overflow paint.

8 • Let dry for 24-48 hours. Remove the tape.

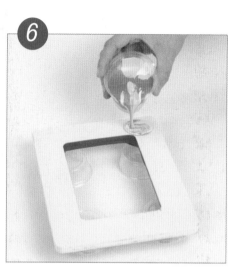

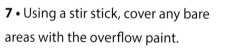

CELESTIAL *clock*

SHOPPING LIST

- ☐ (1) - 9" Pre-cut Wood Clock Kit
- ☐ (3) - 3 fl. oz. Cups
- ☐ (1) - 5 fl. oz. Cup
- ☐ (3) - Acrylic Paints Prepared For Pouring (see page 8)
  - • 2 fl. oz. Blue
  - • 2 fl. oz. Light Blue
  - • 2 fl. oz. White
- ☐ 100% Silicone Oil - 1 Drop Per Color

1 • Fill the hole with a piece of rolled up painters tape, so that it can be removed later.

2 • Add paints in the cup starting with white. Alternate paint colors in differing amounts.

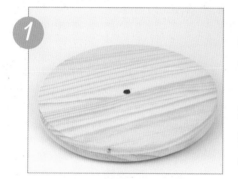

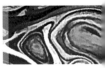

CELESTIAL *clock*

3 • Insert a stir stick into the paint cup and sweep it from one side of the cup to the other, once in each direction, +. This will slightly mingle the paints.

4 • Remove the stir stick and set aside.

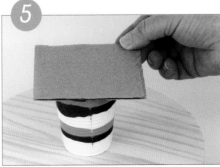

5 • Place a scrap piece of cardboard on top of cup.

6 • Flip cup and cardboard over.

7 • Slide cup off of cardboard onto the clock.

8 • Lift and remove cup.

9 • Tilt canvas until the paint covers the canvas.

10 • Use a stir stick and leftover paint to cover any bare canvas.

11 • Follow the manufacturer's instructions to assemble the clock.

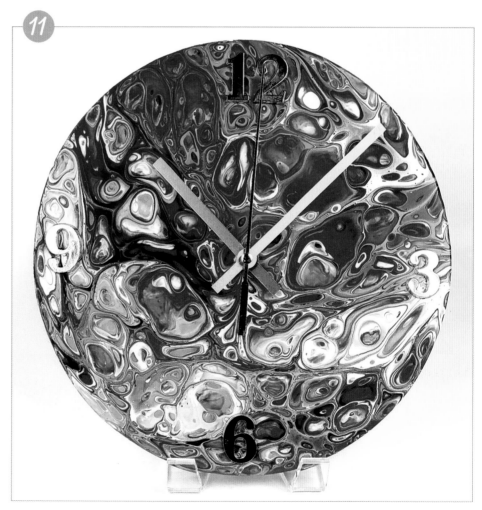

PRINCESS
bow holder

SHOPPING LIST

- ☐ (1) - Crown Shaped MDF Cutout
- ☐ (4) - 3 fl. oz. Cups
- ☐ (1) - 5 fl. oz Cup
- ☐ (4) - Acrylic Paints Prepared For Pouring (see page 8)
  - 2 fl. oz. Iridescent Gold
  - 2 fl. oz. Pink
  - 2 fl. oz. Purple
  - 2 fl. oz. White
- ☐ 100% Silicone Oil - 1 Drop Per Color
- ☐ (3) Cup Hooks
- ☐ ¾ yd Pink Ribbon - 1½" Wide
- ☐ ¾ yd gold Ribbon - ½" Wide
- ☐ Adhesive

INSTRUCTIONS

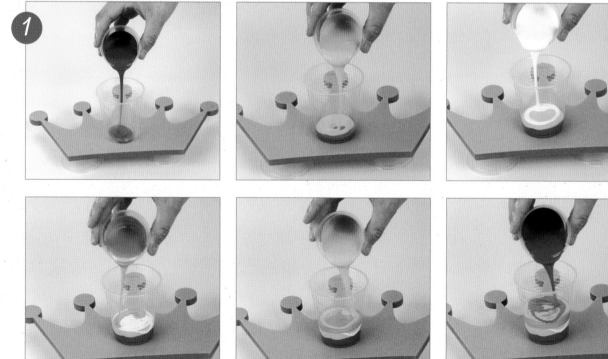

1 • Using the 5 oz. cup, layer the prepared paint colors. Paints can be added in a random order with differing amounts of paint.

PRINCESS *bow holder*

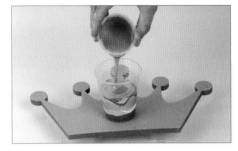

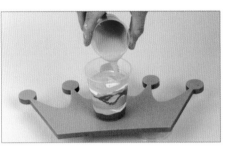
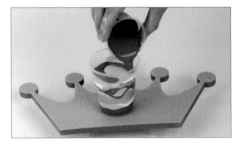

2 • Slowly pour paint across the crown. Tilt the crown until the paint covers the surface.

3 • Use a stir stick to cover edges. Set aside, elevated on two upturned cups to dry for 24-48 hours.

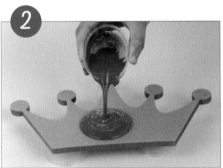

4 • If desired, paint the edges with iridescent gold paint.

5 • Measure your length of ribbon to be twice the width of the crown; cut with scissors.

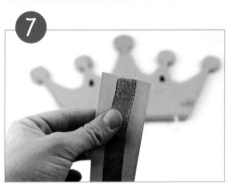

6 • Screw hooks into the bottom of the crown at equal distances.

7 • Glue the gold ribbon over the top of the pink ribbon.

8 • Glue ribbons, right side down, to the back of the crown, at equal distances apart, between the hooks.

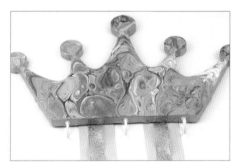

9 • Cut the bottom edges of the ribbon at an angle.

LEISURELY *letters*

SHOPPING LIST

- ☐ (1) Wood Letter
- ☐ (5) - 3 fl. oz. Cups
- ☐ (4) - Acrylic Paints Prepared For Pouring (see page 8)
  - • 2 fl. oz. Blue
  - • 2 fl. oz. Medium Blue
  - • 2 fl. oz. Light Blue
  - • 2 fl. oz. Magenta
- ☐ 100% Silicone Oil - 1 Drop Per Color

INSTRUCTIONS

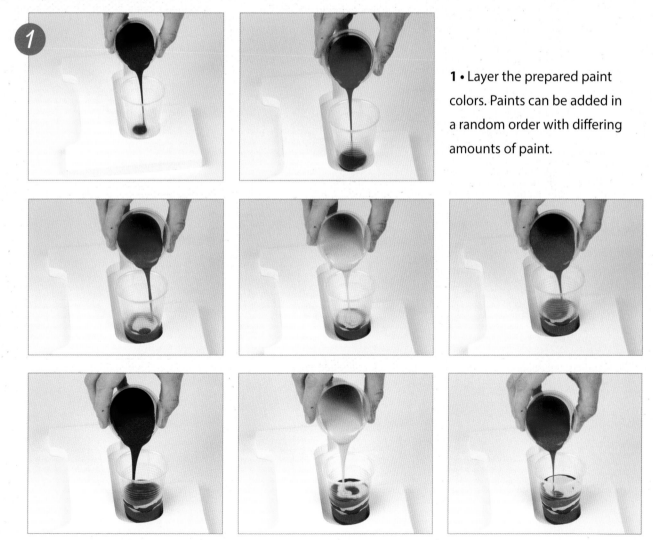

1 • Layer the prepared paint colors. Paints can be added in a random order with differing amounts of paint.

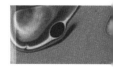

2 • Insert a stir stick into the paint cup and sweep it from one side of the cup to the other, once in each direction, +. This will slightly mingle the paints.

3 • Slowly pour paint across the letter.

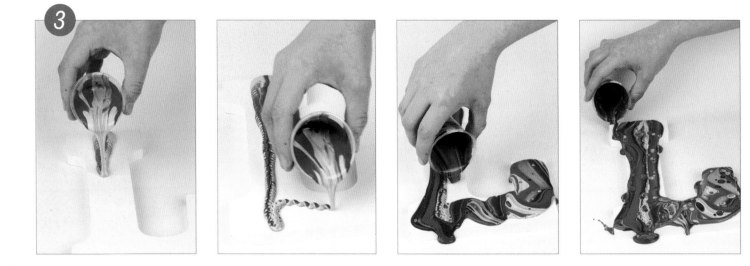

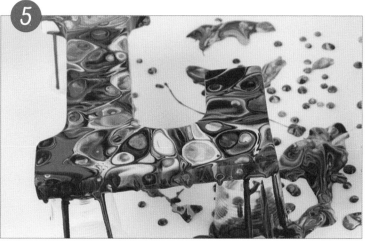

4 • Tilt the letter until the paint covers the surface. Use a stir stick to cover edges.

5 • Set aside, elevated on upturned cups to dry for 24-48 hours.

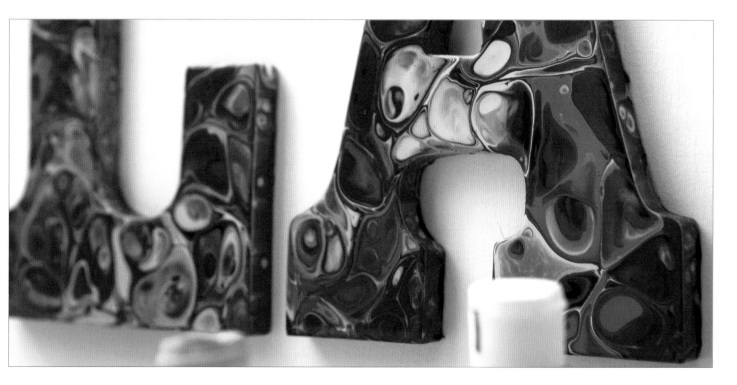

how to FINISH YOUR PAINTING

Adding a clear, protective sealant top coat, spray or brush-on, is a popular way to finish a dry paint pour. It's not a necessity, but it can help to bring back some of the vibrancy and shine that is lost when acrylic paint dries. It will also provide a water-resistant barrier from dirt and other debris that might settle on the surface and need to be cleaned off.

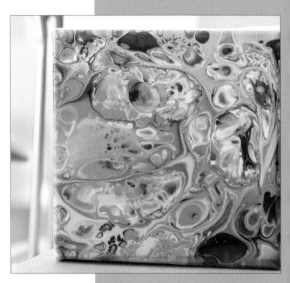

It's best to allow your paintings to cure for 2 - 4 weeks before sealing. This allows time for all the moisture in the paint to evaporate, which might cause your sealant to crack or become cloudy.

What to look for in a sealant:
1 • Water-based
2 • Non-yellowing
3 • Self-leveling
4 • Glossy

Always consult the sealant manufacturer's recommendations on how to apply. Most products will require several thin layers.

If additives like silicone oil are added to the prepared paints, any oily residue left after drying needs to be removed before sealing. Spot cleaning with a gentle household cleaner will usually do the trick.

TROUBLESHOOTING

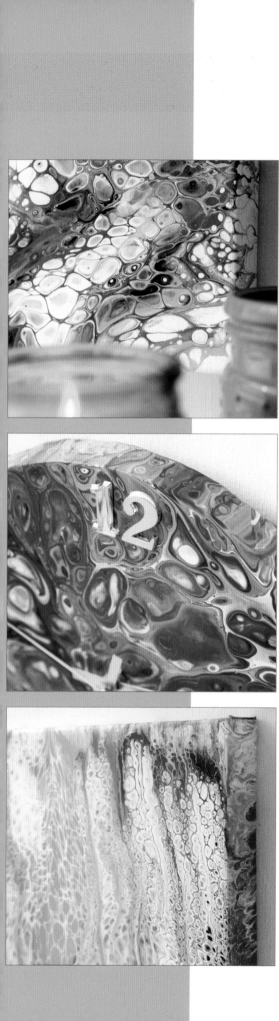

Why do my colors look muddy? How can I keep my reds from turning pink? Colors are going to mix together no matter what you do. You can keep this to a minimum by not making your paints too thin, and not layering certain colors next to each other. The more colors you add into the equation the more likely you are to get brown. If you don't want pink on your canvas, don't layer red and white next to each other. Try layering a different color in between them. Keep color theory in mind, and do your research on different pigments and how they react next to each other, both physically and visually. This can help you achieve the visual effects that you are looking for in your work.

My painting is dry, but now it's cracked! What happened? The things most likely to cause cracking are paints being applied too thick and heavy, air temperature, and applying additional coatings without sufficient curing time.

Some lower quality white paints will often crack no matter what steps you take to avoid it.

When all else fails, Swipe! Oftentimes, a paint pour you're unhappy with can be saved by using the swiping technique over the paint pour you've already started. Not liking what cells you got with that dirty flip cup? Swipe it!

ABOUT THE AUTHOR

Nicky James Burch is an Iowa-born, Southern California-raised artist, now living in North Texas. She has been a practicing visual artist her entire life, and launched Fruit Jar Junction, a renowned quilting studio, in 2000. Her quilting talents in combining textures, color, and design have won her recognition in the industry. She is recognized as a Master Quilter. Being an artist of many interests and talents, Nicky started experimenting with fluid art in 2017. Through experimentation and trial-and-error, Nicky developed her own style with fluid art, including alcohol inks, acrylics, and resin. Nicky's strong interest in technology and sharing, led her to start posting her works and processes on social media, and Fluid Art Studios was born. Nicky is currently showcasing her techniques and pieces on Facebook, YouTube, Instagram and SnapChat. With over 110,000 followers and growing on Facebook's page Fluid Art Studios, she is becoming an international influencer in this relatively new style of artistic expression. She also has created an online community of 40,000 plus fluid artists, called Acrylic Pouring Addiction. She showcases her artistic talents on YouTube, under Nicky James Burch. When she is not creating a new unique piece, she relaxes at home with her husband, three adult children, two grandchildren, and one lucky pet dog, Sherlock.

www.fluidartsupplies.com

You Tube Nicky James Burch

f Fluid Art Studios

f Acrylic Pouring Addiction

 nicky.j.burch

ACKNOWLEDGMENTS

To my family, thank you for supporting me in all of my pursuits and for always encouraging me to follow my dreams. I am especially grateful for my daughter, Lauren LaRee, whose assistance was vital in the creation of this book. I'm truly blessed to be surrounded by such amazing and wonderful people who inspire me in my life.

Made in USA.

Library of Congress Control Number: 2018945163

Production Team: Technical Editor – Lisa Lancaster; Associate Technical Editor – Mary Sullivan Hutcheson; Senior Graphic Designer – Lora Puls; Graphic Designer – Lori S. Malkin; Photo Stylist – Lori Wenger; Photographer – Jason Masters.